I0878786

Searchlight BOOKS™

The Kids' Guide to Government

How Voting and Elections Work

Zelda Wagner

Lerner Publications ◆ Minneapolis

Lerner Publications Company
An imprint of Lerner Publishing Group, Inc.
241 First Avenue North
Minneapolis, MN 55401 USA

For reading levels and more information, look up this title at www.lernerbooks.com.

Main body text set in Adrianna Regular.
Typeface provided by Chank.

Library of Congress Cataloging-in-Publication Data

Names: Wagner, Zelda, 2000– author.
Title: How voting and elections work / Zelda Wagner.
Description: Minneapolis, MN : Lerner Publications, [2025] | Series: Searchlight books. The kids' guide to government | Includes bibliographical references and index. | Audience: Ages 8–11 | Audience: Grades 4–6 | Summary: "Voting and elections are an important part of US democracy. Young readers discover who can vote and how they help elect people to represent them locally and nationally. Learn more about the US government"— Provided by publisher.
Identifiers: LCCN 2023038151 (print) | LCCN 2023038152 (ebook) | ISBN 9798765626597 (library binding) | ISBN 9798765629659 (paperback) | ISBN 9798765637289 (epub)
Subjects: LCSH: Voting—United States—Juvenile literature. | Elections—United States—Juvenile literature.
Classification: LCC JK1978 .W34 2025 (print) | LCC JK1978 (ebook) | DDC 324.973—dc23/eng20230914

LC record available at https://lccn.loc.gov/2023038151
LC ebook record available at https://lccn.loc.gov/2023038152

Manufactured in the United States of America
1-1009927-51990-10/24/2023

Table of Contents

Chapter 1

ELECTION DAY

Tuesday, November 3, 2020, was an exciting day. Voters in the United States were voting for the president. The top candidates were Joe Biden and Donald Trump. Biden had been a vice president and a senator. Trump, then the president, was a real estate business owner.

Voters made their decision. Some voted in person on Election Day or before. Some had their ballots mailed to them and mailed them back or dropped them off.

It took days to count all the ballots. When all were counted, Biden was declared the winner. He was elected the forty-sixth president of the United States.

Biden speaks after being elected president in 2020.

Voters wait in line to cast their ballots in 2020.

The People Decide

US voters can cast their ballots on Election Day. It is on a Tuesday in early November. People vote for the president every four years. They vote for other politicians every two, four, or six years. Every Election Day is different, but the results are always exciting. Nobody knows who will win until the election votes are counted. It is up to the people who vote.

MANY PEOPLE GET A STICKER AFTER VOTING.

Chapter 2

WHY WE VOTE

The US is a representative democracy. The people run a democracy. In US elections, the people vote for the leaders who will represent them. Voting gives people power in their government. Elected leaders know they must do what is best for the people. If they do not do their job well, people might not vote for them in the next election.

Government Branches

The US government has three branches, or parts. They are the legislative, judicial, and executive branches. The president is the leader of the executive branch. It carries out laws. Congress is the legislative branch. It makes the laws. People vote to elect members of Congress to represent their state and district in national government. The judicial branch makes sure the Constitution is followed. Members of the judicial branch are chosen by elected officials.

Congress meets in 2022.

Sarah Huckabee Sanders became the governor of Arkansas in 2023.

Electing State and Local Leaders

People also vote for local leaders in elections. They vote for the leader of the state government. This person is called the governor. States have their own group of lawmakers. They are state senators and state representatives.

Elections also help decide the leaders of a city or town government. There are many other types of elected leaders. For example, people can vote for members of the school board or park board. These leaders help make decisions about schools and parks.

Karen Bass was elected mayor of Los Angeles, California, in 2022.

Who Can Vote?

US citizens must be eighteen years of age or older to vote. They need to register, or sign up, to vote. They must live in their voting area. In some states, voters must also prove who they are by showing identification before they vote.

SOME AREAS ALLOW ONLINE VOTER REGISTRATION.

Deep Dive

When the US first formed, only white men who owned property could vote. Later, white men who didn't have property were allowed to vote. In 1870, Black men won the right to vote. But many states tried to prevent them from voting with poll taxes and literacy tests. In 1920, white women won the right to vote. Four years later, Native Americans were allowed to vote. In 1952, Asian people won the right to vote. In 1965, the Voting Rights Act made it illegal to stop other people from voting. Then more Black women and Latinx people were able to vote.

Chapter 3

THE ELECTION

Candidates work hard to get people to vote for them. They hold meetings and give speeches. They may also hand out flyers, run ads on television, post messages on social media, send emails, or text voters. They tell voters what they plan to do if elected.

People who like a candidate might help them. The supporters also work hard to get other people to vote for their candidate.

Candidates often participate in debates. In a debate, the candidates talk about important issues. They explain how they would solve problems in the nation and in their community. Candidates might have different views about the problems. People watching can decide which candidate they agree with.

Senator Kamala Harris (*left*) and Vice President Mike Pence (*right*) debate in 2020.

Join the Party!

Most candidates are members of a political party. Political parties are made up of people who have similar ideas and goals for the government. The party helps support candidates in elections. The two largest parties in the United States are the Democratic Party and the Republican Party. Smaller parties are called third parties. Some candidates do not belong to any party. They are independent candidates.

Senator Bernie Sanders is the longest-serving independent in Congress.

An election worker checks a voter in at a polling place.

Primary Elections

Many candidates might want to be elected to serve in the government. Smaller elections, called primary elections, are held earlier to shorten the list of candidates. People vote in these primary elections to decide which candidates they like best from each political party. Candidates hope to win enough votes in the primary elections to run in the final election in November.

After people vote in primary elections, political parties decide which candidates they plan to support. Usually, parties support the candidates that won in the primary elections. These decisions are announced at conventions. The two biggest conventions for a presidential election are the Republican National Convention and the Democratic National Convention. Supporters gather at conventions to hear which candidates they might vote for in November.

President Trump talks during the 2020 Republican National Convention.

Democracy and You

You might not be able to vote yet, but you can still make a difference. You can remind friends and family members who are eighteen years old and older to vote. You can also help them make a plan for how they will vote. They could vote in person on Election Day or before. Each state has different voting laws. Together, you can look at websites for federal and state elections. They will tell you how to register and vote.

Election Day

On Election Day, voters might cast their ballots at a polling place. It may be in a public building such as a school or fire station. People working at the polling place get it ready for voters. The workers check that each voter is voting in the right place.

Each voter gets a ballot. A ballot may be a sheet of paper, a card, or an electronic form with a list of the

A POLL WORKER TELLS A PERSON WHERE TO GO TO VOTE.

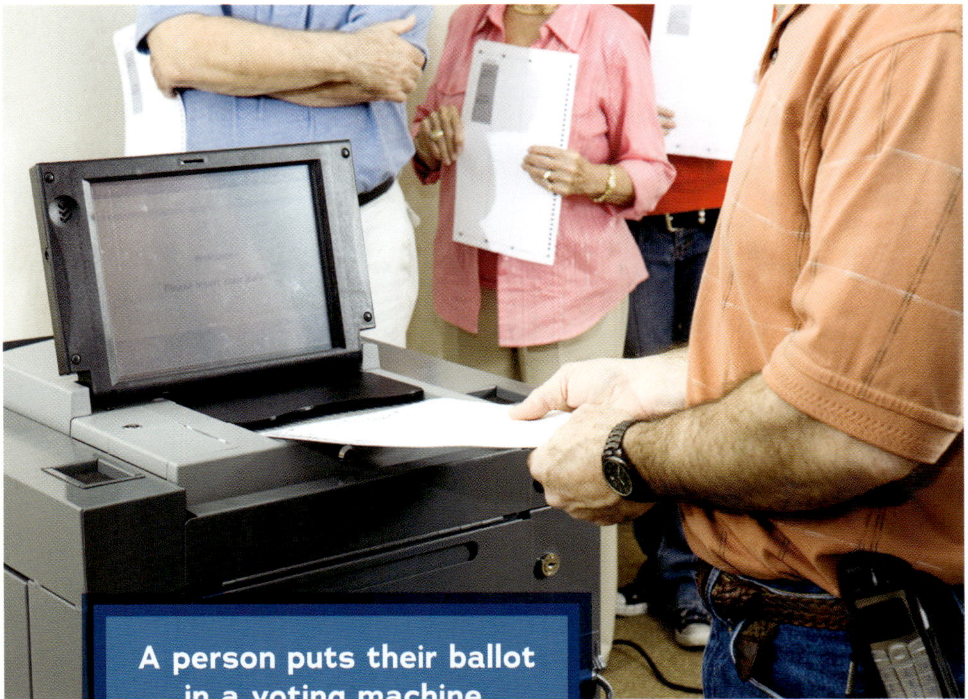

A person puts their ballot in a voting machine.

candidates. Voters show which candidates they want to vote for by marking their names on the ballot in private. They do not see other people's ballots. In some states, voters can send their ballots in the mail before Election Day. Voters can also go to polling places before the election at certain times.

Counting the Votes

At the end of Election Day, the votes from every polling place are counted. Usually the winners are announced on election night. If an election is very close, it may take longer to count the votes. This happened in 2000, when candidates Al Gore and George W. Bush were running for president. The election was so close that votes had to be recounted many times before the winner was announced more than a month after the election.

The Electoral College

In many elections, a candidate wins by getting the most votes. This is the popular vote. A presidential election

Publications after the 2000 presidential election

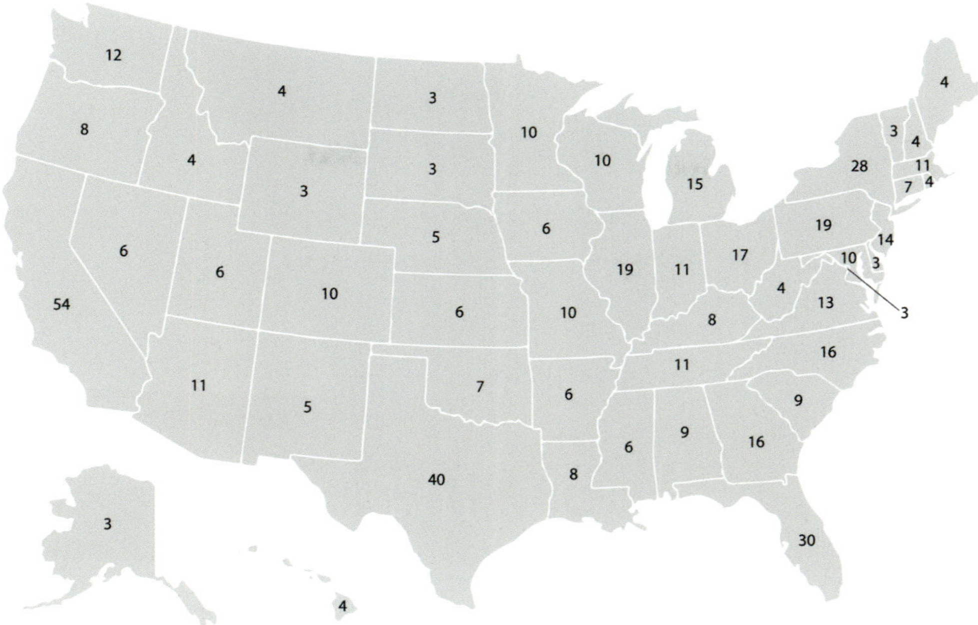

A map of the US that shows how many electoral votes each state has

is different. People vote on Election Day to pick which candidate they like as president. Then the Electoral College, a smaller group of people, votes for a president.

The Electoral College has electors in each state. Electors vote in December. The number of electors in each state depends on the number of people who live in that state. Electors are supposed to vote for the candidate who wins the most votes in their community. To win the election, the candidate must win a majority of the votes cast by the Electoral College.

Deep Dive

A president can win the most votes in the popular vote and still lose the election. This has happened five times in US history: in 1824, 1876, 1888, 2000, and 2016. Each time, the winner of the election got fewer votes overall but was able to win more votes in the Electoral College. For example, in 2016, Hillary Clinton won the popular vote, but Trump had more electoral votes.

Chapter 4

GET INVOLVED

During election years, some schools hold their own elections. Students can cast their own votes at school. These votes are not counted officially, but students get to practice voting. They may compare the results at their own school to the results of the official election.

Students vote in a classroom.

Voting in School

Many schools have a student government. The student government might help organize special events. They can help make changes that students want to see at school. Often students get to vote on candidates for their student government.

There may be other votes at school. For example, students may vote on what type of animal to get for a class pet.

Other Ways to Get Involved

Even if they can't vote, students can get involved in an election. Students can encourage adults to vote. They can support a candidate for office by making signs or talking to people about issues. Students can also get together as a group to show support for an important issue.

You can make a sign to remind people to vote.

A good way to become involved in government is to take part in issues that affect your community. Neighborhoods often have organizations to make the community cleaner and safer. Volunteering for a community organization is a good way to learn how politics works. Even if you can't vote, you can do a lot to help your community and nation.

You can make a difference through volunteering.

What Do You Think?

Some people think kids under eighteen should be able to vote. Some do not. Some argue that kids won't know enough to vote. Kids in school are still learning about how government works. People are worried kids may not understand issues well enough to make a good decision. But if kids voted, politicians might pay more attention to issues that impact younger people, such as education and school safety. They might listen to kids and hear new ideas.

Who is right? Are children under eighteen too young to vote? Why or why not?

Glossary

ballot: a card, sheet of paper, or electronic form used to cast votes in an election

candidate: a person who runs in an election

district: an area or section of a city or nation

Electoral College: a group of people who cast the deciding votes for the US president

political party: a group of people who share similar ideas and goals for government

politician: a person who takes an active part in politics or in government

polling place: the place where people go to cast their votes

primary election: an election held before the final election to narrow down the list of candidates

Learn More

Britannica Kids: Democracy
https://kids.britannica.com/kids/article/democracy/352935

Britannica Kids: Voting
https://kids.britannica.com/kids/article/voting/400199

Chang, Kirsten. *Voting.* Minneapolis: Bellwether Media, 2022.

Ducksters: US Government
https://www.ducksters.com/history/us_government/democracy.php

Lombardo, Jennifer. *What Are Voting Rights?* New York: KidHaven, 2022.

Wagner, Zelda. *How the Legislative Branch Works.* Minneapolis: Lerner Publications, 2025.

Index

Photo Acknowledgments

Image credits: Tasos Katopodis/Getty Images, p. 5; Trevor Bexon/Shutterstock, p. 6; LPETTET/Getty Images, p. 7; JIM WATSON/Getty Images, p. 9; Bloomberg/Getty Images, p. 10; AP Photo/Ted Soqui/SIPA USA, p. 11; Rawpixel.com/Shutterstock, p. 12; Kim Raff/Bloomberg/Getty Images, p. 15; Anna Moneymaker/Getty Images, pp. 16, 17; Jeenah Moon/Bloomberg/Getty Images, p. 18; David Becker for The Washington Post/Getty Images, p. 20; Lisa F. Young/Shutterstock, p.21; HENNY RAY ABRAMS/AFP/Getty Images, p. 22; Independent Picture Service, p. 23; 10'000 Hours/Getty Images, p. 26; SDI Productions/Getty Images, p. 27; Hero Images/Getty Images, p. 28.

Cover: Joaquin Corbalan P/Shutterstock.